ON WINGS OF PROMISE, Vol.1

A Testimony Of God's Faithfulness

Content

DEDICATION

To my father and mother Bitsong Moïse and Mbéké
Bernadette, for laying
down their lives to raise eight children with extremely
limited means.
To my wife Hermine Ebala and our daughter
Shekinah
Dorcas Moukon for their inspiration and
encouragement

THANK YOU

To Judy Free for all the time spent reading, correcting
and editing my manuscript. This work wouldn't have
been published without your wonderful help and
encouragement.

Wordclay
1663 Liberty Drive, Suite 200
Bloomington, IN 47403
www.wordclay.com

First published by Wordclay on 10/28/2008.

ISBN: 978-1-6048-1454-5 (sc)

Printed in the United States of America.

This book is printed on acid-free paper.

INTRODUCTION

There are moments in our lives that we can't hide, but must bring them to the attention of the public. There are experiences that we can't just keep for ourselves, like holding a piece of truth in the museum of our brain and selfishly resisting the temptation to let them out, that they might profit withal. The resistance sometimes comes from the fact that we don't recognize the God-given gift in our lives and the supernatural power that we have received from the Holy Spirit to "be my [Jesus'] witnesses in Jerusalem and in all Judea and Samaria and to the end of the earth." (Acts 1:8-RSV). Really it is not us, but God. Some discovered the gifts of God in their lives and immediately started acting upon them, but without too much conviction and enthusiasm, that are interwoven in our faith. Their faith took a substantial leap when, following the advice of a friend, they went back to their study and began digging into their souls again to recapture the excitement of early days, to communicate by ink and paper, what they'd almost lost. After attempting many times to write for publication I failed, until now. Under the motivation

1

of a friend, who wrote to me just a few weeks after my arrival in the United States of America and the help of God I am happy that today the long striving years have finally paid off.

On Wings Of Promise has been written as a contribution to the many publications out there related to the blessings and the faithfulness of God. In this book I am giving an account of God's work around, in, and through my life starting with my home country. I also give a highlight about the village where I was born. Family values are almost never forgotten in every piece of writing presented by a native African, whether it is directly or indirectly spoken of. The importance of education is never going to be emphasized enough.

Through their sacrifices, my parents taught me how serious they looked on the acquisition of knowledge and God taught me how valuable my life was to Him. The assurance of eternal life is a powerful truth and divine revelation that every human being can have. When I think about soul winning and the context of <u>Acts1:8</u>, I believe that God wanted me to witness, after receiving the power first in "Jerusalem" which in application is my country- Cameroon. And that's what I did before landing in "Judea".

2

Chapter One
CAMEROON IN A NUTSHELL
Early history

From archeological evidence it is known that humans have inhabited Cameroon for at least 50, 000 years, and there is strong evidence of the existence of important kingdoms and states in more recent times. Of these, the most widely known is Sao, which arose in the vicinity of Lake Chad, probably in the 5th century AD. This kingdom reached its height from the 9th to the 15th centuries, after which it was conquered and destroyed by Kotoko state, which extended over large portions of northern Cameroon and Nigeria. Kotoko was incorporated into Bornu Empire during the reign of Rabih az-Zubayr (Rabah) in the late 19th century, and its people became Muslims.

The Name

Cameroon is one of the more than 40 countries that the continent of Africa is made of. History says that the name "Cameroon" derived from the Portuguese word, Camaroes, meaning shrimps. A Portuguese sailor Fernão do Pó in 1472 arrived at the River Wouri in Douala, at the coast of the country and discovered so many shrimps in the river that he decided to call it "Rio Dos Camaroes" which means "River of shrimps, in Portuguese". It was from this word that the territory derived its name, which is now spelt in various forms: Spanish spelt it Cameroes; German, Kamerun; English, Cameroon; and French, Cameroun.

Colonization and consequences

The Germans colonized the territory in 1884 and after the end of the 1914-1918 war, Cameroon was mandated by the League Nations (later United Nations trusts) to the French and British governments. France took the greater sector, formally known as East Cameroon, while Britain took responsibility over former West Cameroon known then as "Cameroon under British Administration."

The British trust territory consisted of a strip of land bisected by the Bénoué River along the eastern border of Nigeria. British rule was a period of neglect. This, coupled with the influx of numerous Nigerians caused great resentment.

The French territory had an administration based on that of the other territories of French Equatorial Africa.

Although there were differences in the French and British colonial experiences, there were also strong similarities. Most important, these rulers continued drawing Cameroon into the international economic system. By the time of independence, the trusts produced raw materials for Europe, and especially France, for the finished goods. This fragile economy continues to plague Cameroon.

Independence And Ramifications

After World War II, developments in Cameroon and Europe brought about independence. On January 01, 1960 the French Sector became independent under the new name of Cameroon Republic. Following agitation for independence by the Southern Cameroons-before the name was changed to West Cameroon-a plebiscite was held in that sector of Cameroon on February 11th 1961 under the United Nations supervision. The result of the plebiscite that was overwhelming for reunification (133,571 against 97,741) gave Southern Cameroons automatic independence and unification, which was achieved on October 1st 1961. Thus after the reunification of both sectors, the Federal Republic of Cameroon was born.

After a May 20, 1972 referendum, Cameroon became a United Republic and by a Presidential Decree of 1984 it became the Republic of Cameroon, as we will see later on. The above-mentioned dates are very important for the Country of Cameroon. Every February 11th and May 20th is a day of celebration for the population of Cameroon every year.

Economy

Cameroon Liberalism Planned under Ahidjo was formulated to encourage private investment, with government to play a strong role in guiding development. Expansion of export crops was to provide the foreign capital needed. In the 1973 announcement of the Green Revolution, the government proposed that country was to become self-sufficient in food and to become the primary food source for its neighbors.

The discovery of exploitable petroleum in the 1970s was a great boost to the economy, and petroleum became the most valuable export. Petroleum revenues were used to increase prices to farmers, to pay for imports of materials and technology and to build financial reserves. Sadly petroleum income also paid for expensive, badly planned projects.

Large-scale industrial development projects met with little success. Problems in planning, technology transfer, and market research plagued these projects, and much capital was lost. There were more medium-sized enterprises producing goods for local use. But to a large extent the country still depended on imported industrial goods. Exceptions to this were refined petroleum products, cement, textiles and clothing, beverages, and aluminum. Expansion of transportation facilities, the development of hydroelectric capability, and tremendous growth in education took place.

Ahidjio resigned just before a severe economic crisis emerged, and Cameroonians placed the blame on Biya. The crisis was the result of international economic conditions and the dependent economy he inherited. Decreases in commodity prices were harmful. Cameroon's income, dependent on exports, dropped. In 1987 Biya admitted that the country faced an economic crisis. A World Bank structural adjustment program and budget cuts were necessary, and ripple effects were felt throughout the economy. While Cameroon had made economic progress since independence, it had not been able to change the dependant nature of its economy. This realization was the cause of much frustration, and in the late 1980s opposition to the government grew.

Here are some facts to look at. **Natural resources**: Oil, timber, hydroelectric power, natural gas, and cobalt, nickel. **Agricultural products**: timber, coffee, tea, bananas, cocoa, rubber, palm oil, pineapples, cotton. **Industries**: Petroleum production and refining, aluminum production, food processing, light consumer goods, textiles, lumber, ship repairs. The following partners contribute to the economy of Cameroon. **Exports partners**: Spain 17.2%, Italy 13.7%, France 9.4%, South Korea 8.1%; UK 8%, Netherlands 7.8%, Belgium 4.8%, USA 4.3 % (2005 statistics). **Imports partners:** France 25%, Nigeria 12.5%; Belgium 6.6 %, China 5.8%, USA 5.3%, Thailand 4.7%, Germany 4.4% (2005 statistics). Currency: Communauté Financière Africaine (CFA)-franc (XAF)

Politics And Administration

The first nationalist party, the Cameroon

People's Union (UPC) led by Felix-Roland Moumie and Reuben Um Nyobe, demanded a thorough break with France and the construction of a socialist economy. French officials suppressed the UPC, leading to a bitter civil war, while encouraging alternative political leaders. On January 1st, 1960, independence was granted, with Ahmadou Ahidjo the first president. Ahidjo and his party, the Cameroon Union, pledged to build a capitalist economy and to maintain close ties to France.

Ahidjio ruled from independence until 1982. He centralized power in the capital, Yaoundé, and in one person—himself. Cameroon became an authoritarian, single-party in which civil rights meant little. The civil war ended slowly and brutally, but the state of emergency continued for years beyond its conclusion. Ahidjo declared nation building to be a major goal using the fear of ethnic conflict to justify authoritarianism.

In 1982 Cameroon underwent a dramatic political change, and important though less obvious economic changes were under way. On November 4th President Ahidjo resigned the presidency, and two days later Paul Biya took power. Paul Biya took office on 11/06/1982 and became the first elected president in the history of Cameroon. He changed the United Republic of Cameroon into the Republic of Cameroon. He created a new political party to replace the Cameroon National Union, the Cameroon People

Democratic Movement (CPDM). Paul Biya has been the national president of the country's ruling party since his election to the supreme magistracy.

Biya sought the development of a more democratic society. Although the country was still a single-party state, he allowed competitive elections for party offices and the National Assembly. He also experimented with freedom of speech and the press.

From 7 States, the new administrative divisions with the new president since 1990 brought the number to 10. Those States and their headquarters are as follow

- North   Headquarters   Maroua
- Adamawa   Headquarters   Ngaoundéré
- Center Headquarters   Yaoundé
- South   Headquarters   Ebolowa
- Littoral   Headquarters   Douala
- East   Headquarters   Bertoua
- West   Headquarters   Bafoussam
- South-East   Headquarters   Buéa
- North-West   Headquarters   Bamenda
- Far-North   Headquarters   Garoua

Each of these States has its individual features and is mainly characterized by its culture; where the language, I mean the national language and the inhabitants' social activities take a very important place.

Like every country in the world Cameroon has a flag: Green, Red with a golden star in the middle and Yellow. Green represents the southern part of the country where a lot of agricultural activities take place. The yellow color is a sign of hope coming from the sunshine. The sun rises up in the East of the country, many people believe. The red color is the symbol of martyrdom: the blood that was shed by our founding fathers as they fought for independence.

Geographical Location And Border Countries

Cameroon is the only African country with a shape easy to identify from the African map. She is located in Central West Africa, a little bit on top of the equator, bordering the Bight of Biafra (part of the Gulf of Guinea and the Atlantic Ocean). Area: 475 000 sq.km. (184 000 sq.mi). Terrain: Northern plains, central and western highlands, southern and coastal tropical forests. Highest peak: Mt. Cameroon (13,353 ft.). Cameroon shares her borders in the South with the Equatorial Guinea. In the North she shares her borders with the Republic of Chad. In the East with Central African Republic, and Congo and in the West with Nigeria. When you move inside Cameroon from any of those borders you will be welcome by her seasons' diversities.

Climate And People

Like most of African countries we find four

seasons in Cameroon. Two dry seasons and two rainy seasons that alternate. In these divisions, there is one heavy dry season and a small dry season. There is also one heavy rainy season and the small rainy season. Northern plains, the Sahel region—semiarid and hot (7-month dry season); Central and western highlands where Yaoundé is located—cooler, shorter dry season; southern tropical forest—warm, 4 month dry season; Coastal tropical forest, where Douala is located—warm, humid year-round. Since Cameroon is a tropical country where those seasons alternate you would therefore like to know when to come and visit, and which part of Cameroon you would like to discover first.

The people of Cameroon are Cameroonians: French noun and adjective—Camerounais (e). The population, from 2003 estimate is 16.5 million (52% in rural areas).

Although Cameroon is a bilingual country-French and English being the two official languages we find about 270 African languages and dialects, including pidgin, Fulfude, and Ewondo. There are about 250 ethnic groups. The literacy counts for 75%. It is what makes some historians and learned people say that Cameroon is a country of culture and language diversity. And in addition to that, the country strives for tolerance, solidarity, and human rights respect. Wherever you are in Cameroon you will be attracted by peoples' way of life, peoples' interests, and peoples' culture, which are different from what you watch everywhere else.

Religion

Islam became a powerful force in the northern and central portions of the country through conquest, immigration, and the spread of commerce from north and northwestern Africa. The most significant bearers of this faith the Fulani entered northern Cameroon beginning in the 18th century. The host populations welcomed the first small groups of pastoralists. Eventually the Fulani, frustrated under non-Muslim rule and encouraged by the teachings of the mystic Usman dan Fodio, revolted. In the early 1800s Modibbo Adama was appointed by Usman to lead a jihad over large areas centered in northern Nigeria, which were incorporated into Usman's Sokoto Empire. The Fulani conquest was brief and did not result in Islamization, although later ruler, Sultan Njoya, accepted this faith in the early 20th century.

Christian missionaries were also becoming a factor. Under the leadership of Alfred Saker, a Briton, and West Indians such as Joseph Merrick, a Baptist station was established in 1845 at Akwa Town (now Douala). Saker established a large post at Victoria (now Limbe) in 1858. The American Presbyterian mission opened a station in 1871. The origin and denomination of the missions changed frequently, but the Presbyterians, Baptists, and Roman Catholics have been the most important. Statistics show the

12

following: Christian 53%, Muslim 22%, and indigenous African 25%.

It is said that Cameroon is Africa in miniature. The main reason is that the culture the country presents, the agricultural diversity especially, is found in all the other African countries. The country welcomes people from every other country of Africa and lives in perfect solidarity and harmony with them. Thus being a sort of melting pot inside the African continent, Cameroon still keeps her status of "Africa in miniature."

The motto of the country is "Peace-Work-Fatherland."

Two important administrative cut I would like to mention here are: Cities and Counties. I am mainly going to speak about the Cities and Counties from the Center State where the State Capital of Cameroon is located. Besides, it is in that province that I was born.

In descending order, Cities become Counties, and Counties become Districts. The Districts are scattered into villages.

Going To My City of birth, Ntui

The City I was born in is called Ntui. It is found in the Mbam and Kim County and my City is the headquarters of this County. It was a village before. The City-Ntui- is situated about 50 miles away from Yaoundé, the State Capital. The population, according the recent statistics I found is about 6,185 inhabitants. The geographical coordinates are as follows: 4 ° 27' 0" North, 11°38'00" East. The means of transportation when you want to get to my village is by car or bush taxis or bush buses.

The journey takes four hours and sometimes more due to the quality of the roads. The roads that go to my village are bumpy. If you traveled during the rainy season, you would be confronted with a muddy and sliding road that would not always make the trip easy.

Sometimes the bus would be stuck in the mud with passengers on board. The driver would then ask everyone to step out of the vehicle and push it. Not every passenger would be asked to push. Women and children as well as senior citizens would be exempt from this task, which would require only young men's power. Patience, prayer and jokes would animate such journeys, be they in the rainy season or the dry season.

The dry season like the rainy season also has its challenges. The main problem is the dust, because the road is not tarred. The dust would enter the bus through the windows and the old broken doors, and blow everywhere in the bus making it hard to breathe. When the careless passengers took no precaution they would reach their destination completely covered with dust from head to toe. Their face would look like a monster. Their hair, which was once black, would turn red.

There would be no sign on the road to inform you that you were getting close to Ntui except some old acacia trees, old colonial houses and the first Presbyterian Church in which I was raised.

Chapter Two
FAMILY VALUES, ACTIVITIES AND CHALLENGES

My mother, Mbéké Bernadette, used to go farming, but due to the fact that she became sick, she instead had to stay home or reduce the intensity of her farming activities. The greatest part of our food came from my mother's farm. In fact she had three very large fields.

The first one, carried the following well-known names in the capital of my country: "Etat Major". This name was given to locate the closest field to the house.

The next field was nicknamed "Mont Fébé", because this field was further than "Etat Major" and the furthest field was nicknamed "Kondengui."

That field was not only the farthest of all, but also the soil there was not as soft as the others. Note therefore that "kondengui" is the biggest prison in of our nation's capital. If my mother gave that name to the furthest field it was to identify the suffering we endured there to the one you would have to face in the prison of "kondengui" itself.

"Kondengui" was characterized by its lack of shelter, the roughness of its soil, wild animals and birds that would attack the crop. The most difficult farming work was carried out at "kondengui" like growing yams, sweet potatoes and cucumbers.

Despite of this entire frightening picture she presented, we still enjoyed going to "kondengui" because my little brother and I liked to carry each other in a wheelbarrow while walking the long distance from the house to the "prison". By doing that we would forget the hard and painful work that awaited my brothers, my sister and me.

They laid down their lives

I was born in a family of 8 children. There were 7 boys and 1 girl. My brothers Tobé Roger (passed away a few years ago); he was the elder of the family. After him is Mbassa Henry, then Jean Claude Mabeng. The next one, Nkemi Alphonse (passed away). After him is the princess, Awondjena Sylvie, Bertrand Nsan Leon, myself David Moukon and the last, but not the least, Marcel Ndzié. As you can see the men have taken dominion and authority with love in my family. Maybe that's the reason why my dad had to impose his authority also to succeed in his responsibility as a father.

My father's name's Moïse Bitsong. He was a corn factory operator. He owned that factory for many years. He had inherited it from his brother-in law whose name I carry today. That machine was used to process corn, the first consumed food in town. The reputation of my father expanded in town thanks to this job which would draw many people, essentially women, elderly women, when they would not send their children, even if they had one. When they did not have any, they would just call the son of their concubine or neighbor and send him. According to the African tradition children don't only belong to their genitors, they belong to the community.

Sometimes during the holidays or on weekends I would go to my father's factory to watch him work in the midst of a constant smoke and loud noise.

To start the engine, my dad would continuously pull a leather rope as hard as he could, from front to back until the engine would start. Then quickly he would turn to the other side of the engine where he would pour the corn to be processed in a large container which was linked to the grain processor after the grains have passed through my dad's fingers and the processor's mouth.

The final result was a corn flour. Not all the customers were satisfied with the quality of the flour. So my dad would start the whole process again. Generally, it was after this that the customers would express their satisfaction and pay.

The other clients would sit on a long bench after they had measured their corn and cassava and put their bag or bucket in line. They would wait as the line moved slowly.

My dad would sometimes work until late at night under a dim light of a traditional lamp that he would send someone to come home and get. I would feel sleepy when we would leave the factory to walk home.

My dad's job was a very hard job; almost all my brothers did the same job. My dad was training them. The money that my dad made in that job was used for our education, feeding, clothing and traveling needs. It sometimes makes me cry when I think of the sacrifices my parents made, and how they laid down their lives to raise us up.

I faced that too, but we still loved dad

But still my father would use the money to drink at times. He would sometimes get completely drunk as a result of drinking too much.

That would bring a kind of disorder in my life and the life of my brothers and sister also. The scenario was almost the same all the time.

My father would make his voice heard from the road. When he would find us on the table studying, he would speak so loud, screaming at us, making us lose our concentration and desire to study. Instead of closing our books, we would stay there with our books opened and our eyes fixed on them. I

18

was giving the impression to read under the dim light of the only traditional study lamp we had. But to tell the truth I was no more reading, but just praying that God would take me to my bed at that moment.

None of us could stand up to go to bed. When you tried to do it, my father would ask you where you were going. When you said, to bed, he would ask you to "sit down. I am speaking to you." We were frightened, silent and thoughtful.

My father would shout at my mother, and yell at her. When she was not in the dining room, he would ask her to come and stand before us. We had to wait until my dad had entered his bedroom, before we could leave the living room as quickly as we could, and escape in our rooms, wrapping our little bodies in our blankets hoping not to be called out.

Once in his bedroom with my mother, my father would continue yelling at my mom, abusing her verbally, embarrassing her with questions of nonsense. I quite remember when one day my father accused my mother of adultery. I did not know this word-he used in our language-before. What he was saying was that my mother used to go out and wash the clothes of a medical doctor. My mother would not do such a thing.

My mother would not reply every time to my dad's threat, and accusations, because when she tried to reply, I would hear noises like beatings. In fact my father would start beating on my mom. I could hear her repeat again and again "yes, kill me, kill me." And I would start crying in my bed. Whatever my brothers would say could not prevent me from crying. Like in a movie the scene is so clear in my mind.

When my mom could open the door, she would run out and hide behind the kitchen, which was separated from the main house. My father would go out and continue yelling and looking for her until he would come back into our rooms to wake us up so we could go and look for our mother.

It happened sometimes at 2 or 3 am. We knew we would find her. And when we did, she would whisper to us in our mother tongue "go back to bed". With tears in my eyes I would go to bed with the others. But my mom would stay outside in the dark, when she would not sleep in the kitchen, on the floor or on an uncomfortable bamboo bed.

The following day my mother would not be found in the kitchen or outside. We would find her nowhere. She went to sleep at our aunt's house, a few miles from our home. When she came home, she would stand away from my father. She would not enter the house.

The effect of alcohol deeply affected the life of my father and ours. When my father would speak he never wanted to hear from anybody. I remember that one day he asked me where my mom went. I said that I did not know (with fear) and he slapped me. One day again when he was drunk he started speaking loudly, verbally abusing people and my elder brother who was sitting at the other end of the yard kept replying to him and when he got upset he picked up the only radio that we had and threw it at my brother, but he was able to escape.

Despite all that, we still loved him and we knew also that he loved us. The attention and the protection that we all benefited from him was a clear indication that he loved and cared. I forgive all that he might have done to me and he has forgiven me too. My dad and I are great friends. Keep reading, the next lines will tell you how.

Affected By Poverty: Around The Tables

Like most of the children who were born in the same environment like me, life is basically focused on family values, community interchange, education and religion. The family being the focal point of the society at that time, a lot of attention is being given to the parents. They represent the principal source of provision for the family: food, shelter, clothing, health and education. You certainly want to ask if my parents are able to provide with all the needs of eight children. Or you want to know how two individuals will take care of a family of ten. I believe I would ask the same question too if I were you. But let me tell you this: My parents are not materially or financially rich. They don't have a lot of money. Having a lot of money here meaning being able to afford a complete furnished home with electricity and at least four bedrooms, every education material for all the children. I can still remember that my brother (especially the youngest one) and I have to share books. When I am promoted to the next class/grade I am going to keep my books so that he can use them as soon as he gets to the grade I've just graduated from. We could not even afford the three-course meals everyday. That is one of the common concerns in many families born in the same era like mine. Let me talk about our breakfast.

It is not pancake, scrambled eggs with orange juice and jelly. It is not coffee, nor tea or hot chocolate with milk and sugar. It neither is nor even bread, butter and mayonnaise, or cereal with low fat milk (2%). Our breakfast consists most of the time of the reheated food of our previous day's lunch. It simply means that the food we are having today at lunch is going to be reheated tomorrow morning. And that's what we are going to eat for breakfast before going to school. In some occasions I can say in good/happy days my mother is going to cook some corn pudding for breakfast. We will drink that and eat donuts. Those are very rare and special moments. Our lunch basically made of cassava leaves and boiled cassava roots, when my mother is not cooking "fufu" from cassava flour. This dish provides with vitamins to the body. Our protein supply comes from dry fish "bifaka" soup with very tasty ingredients that only my mother knows how to maneuver upon. We will sometimes eat "bifaka" soup with cassava flour "fufu", or mashed potatoes. We also have yams, sweet potatoes and cassava sticks to accompany the dry fish soup dish.

Fresh fish comes from stores that only sell it in my village. My mom makes some provision every time she can afford some. She cooks a delicious soup of tomatoes, onions and garlic with magi for lunch. Corn "fufu" will most of the time accompany this tasty dish of fresh fish. When it was not vegetables it was dry fish and if it is not dry fish it will be fresh fish and when it is not fresh fish it is meat. Yes, meat. What kind of meat? Cow meat, pork or bush meat like snakes, rats and monkeys. We also had porcupine and dear.

An uncle of mine who travels regularly from another town—Yoko—not far from where I was born to the city supplies bush meat. Every time he takes a trip to the city-Yaoundé-he is going to stop by and bring with him a delicious smoked bush meat dish.

This day is a raining day when there is a knock on the door. I don't remember who is going to open. My uncle—Tata Abanda—is here, from "Yoko" with a cocoa bag and another small bag. There is a smell. The smell fills the house. It smells like dried meat. Yes, the cocoa bag has dried bush meat in it. And how about the other bag? We will see later. We listen to my uncle and my parents exchanging words about his journey, while sitting in the living room with our books opened. They are opened, but we don't want to read any more, because of the smell. Finally "tata Abanda" calls one of us. Most of the time it was I, except I am mistaken. "Open the small bag over there; there is something inside", he says. We knew what was inside. With a lot of excitement I am jumping from my chair and bending on the precious bag to take out a bowl, which is covered. "Please, go and heat that". "Hey, not the bowl, but what is inside", he instructed me.

Inside the bowl is monkey meat. Very quickly I am rushing to the kitchen out of the main house. When it is ready my brothers and my mother help me set the table. One side is reserved for the parents and the other side for the children. I don't eat a lot of pepper, How about you? Well this is a delicious food, but there is a lot of pepper in it and I don't know that.

I am going to start eating the meat. There is pepper I must stop eating. No, this is delicious. I like it. I am eating, but I've not finished eating when my eyes quickly get red and my tongue starts "burning". I cannot help, but let it outside of my mouth like a dog, which has been running all day long without a rest. I feel like there is smoke coming out of my ears and nose. I am in pain, but I am not going to let anybody know. Everybody is still eating like nothing is happening to him or her. I know they feel the pepper too. There is water on the table in a big cup. I have swallowed almost two and a half of the cups. But it is like the pain has been intensified and turned my mouth into a "burning bush". There are big drops of sweat and tears falling from my face and eyes. Am I crying? I do not really know what to say. "There is a lot of pepper", I say. With my nose running and dripping I run to my mom. "There is a lot of pepper", I keep saying. "O, I am sorry, baby", she replies. "I tried water, but it got worse", I will tell her. They finally tell me: "Open your mouth very widely and leave it open at the head of the lamp so that the heat of the lamp might enter your mouth, and the pain will cease. Or take a piece of burning fire wood, open your mouth and let the heat enter it." I almost faced death, that day, by trying all those means of relief. None of them really helped me, but increased the pain. I think I am going to keep my mouth closed because the more I open it to ask for help or assistance, the more I am in pain as the air enters in. People keep asking me, "Are you ok?" "Are you still feeling any pain?" I don't answer. You know why. I am silent until I go to bed.

The House I Was Raised In: Days Of Pains And Sorrows

The family house has been here for years. The wall is made of mud and the roof is made of thatch. The mud has been covered with cement and then painted to give it a nice appearance. But when you consider that a house looses its beauty, as the years go by you should know that my family's house has

25

lost its beauty and resistance as the years passed. Let me mention in passing that we are not the first to occupy this house. The story about how we've come to stay here maybe will come in the next book. But for now this is the family's house. The left side of the house, when you come from the main road or the front door, is falling down. My dad, with the help of some relatives and neighbors will try to support it with pools. That's the side of the house where our bedrooms are. Day after day the wall seems to lean and the pools seem not to be resistant enough to support the weight of the wall. Everyone who passes or walks by says, "This wall is not going to be here in the next couple of days". Surprisingly they find the wall standing a couple of day after their false prophecy. I was very scared nevertheless. But my dad has a plan. He will start building a new wall right behind the old and falling one. As soon as he decides to do so we will help him carry the pools from the forest, where he goes to cut them down, to the house. We don't have a truck, so we have to carry the pools on our heads. The next thing is to dig holes. We will do it and after two or three days the pools and the bamboo trees that are tied to the pools are put together. The bamboo trees that are being lined up on each side of the pools leave a space between them. This space will be filled with stones before the mud is applied on the wall to complete the job. To fill up these spaces we gather dried mud, pieces of rocks or stones. With these materials we will fill up the holes and start preparing the mud that will be applied on the wall.

My dad has found a good ground where we will dig and make mud out of the dirt with a mixture of water. With the help of the young boys of the neighborhood, we begin to work, having fun as we walk on the mud to make it ready for the wall. When this is ready we will carry it the elder who finally apply it to the wall. My mom is as busy as every one else: walking in the mud, carrying it and even applying it to the wall herself. In one day the job is done.

As a reward to our hard work we will sit together and share a meal. My mom cooked before the work began. Everybody is going to eat and thank her. There is so much to eat that we are going to keep the extra for the family. Even if my mom were able to cook and at the same time come to help in the work, she is not easily going to do it when we are replacing the roof of the house. The roof is made of palm tree leaves.

Our house is leaking almost in every corner. In the bedroom of my parents, there are at least five leaking spots/locations. In our bedrooms you can number at least two leaking zones in each bedroom. The living room has two big leaking areas. When it starts raining we begin to locate every leaking place and put a bucket there for water to drop in.

Sometimes the rain is so heavy that the wind that accompanies it blows parts of the roof off and back again. When the roof does not come back into place, there will be a hole on the house. Then water from the rain will just pour down. That actually happened one day.

My younger brother and I are sharing the same bed. It is almost 10 pm and the wind is blowing intensely. I can hear the sound of the wind as it hits the trees and the roof of our bedroom with violence. It is not started to rain yet, but this is a warning. My mom is the first person to stand up. She puts a bucket everywhere there will be a leak. Because we also fetch from the rain, water to drink, to do the dishes, the laundry, to cook and take a bath, she is going to get the necessary buckets ready-larger than every other buckets-and take them out a few minutes after the rain has started falling.

My younger brother and I are blotted under our covers in our beds. The wind continues to blow and this time flipping over the sides of the roof of our bedroom just where our heads are. When that side of the roof opens up with the wind a light flashes in the sky and we hear the thunder. We tremble with fear on our little bed. The wind keeps blowing and flipping the roof over and covering it back again. "Don't let this happen, please," I speak to myself. Suddenly it starts raining and with the rain the wind. This time the wind is going to blow to the point where the roof is taken away leaving the top of the house wide open for the rain to fall straight on our heads. We jump out of our bed quickly as our mom comes to check how we are doing. We are completely wet already. She takes us to their bedroom.

There is water everywhere. My younger brother is going to sleep with my dad and my mom. There is a little bed at the bottom of dad's bed. To be able to sleep in it my mom has to use a large aluminum piece of roof to put over the bed. Actually it is going to be placed on each end of the bed, giving me some room to slide in. The raindrops will fall on "the roof" until dawn. I am not going to sleep at all.

Chapter Three
STUDENT LIFE IN PUBLIC AND PRIVATE INSTITUTIONS, AND FAITH

The difficulties I faced in the environment I was brought up challenged me. And I said to myself "I don't want to stay here any longer" and my elder brother told me that the best way to go way from my dad's "torture" was to pass the "GCE". Thank God, I passed and was getting ready to go and study in a different city, as a high school student now, away from my father.

Academic Challenges In Bafia

Now as a student at the Government High School of Bafia, I had to work hard to succeed in my exams. In fact according to the French Education System I would sit for two exams as a high school student. One in Lower Sixth and that exam was called "probatoire" (The High School Diploma). The second exam that is taken in Upper Sixth is called "Baccalauréat", the baccalaureate diploma or the "Advanced Level" exam. The study environment was not what I was expecting. It was extremely hard for me to find a quiet place in the house where I was living to read my books.

The family compound had three houses. Two, where each of my aunts lived and another one, facing the main road, which rooms students can rent. I don't remember exactly where I began to stay as soon as I got to the city. I think I was staying with my aunt Therese in a three-bedroom house with a kitchen inside and a big living room. In some occasions the cooking would be carried outside. The food was not just cooked for the occupants of the house, but also for some "special guests."

Everything at the house seemed to be fine at the beginning of the school year. I would wake up early every morning to go and fetch drinking water from a close fountain that belonged to neighbor or bathing, cooking and laundry water from a well a few miles from the house. Now seeing all what the water would be needed for you can easily imagine what quantity I would have to go and fetch every morning and evening Monday through Sunday. There was no means of transportation to go and fetch that water. I had to carry on my head one of the largest plastic or steel made buckets that we had in the house, not just for one trip, but also for at least five. The next task after that was to wash the dishes, clean the house and dust the furniture before taking my bath and hit the road to school. In the meantime my aunt would wake up and cook.

At the beginning I never understood why she cooked a lot of food, until one day, when I was already in bed at around 10 pm I heard a lot of noise in the living room. Men voices and a few women voices were heard. And as they were talking, they ate also and even drank. Now I did not know where the beer came from. That really made me feel uncomfortable, not just because they were preventing me from sleeping, but also because of the un-edifying conversations they were holding. I would stay awake until the last customer left. Yes of course I later found out that my aunt was cooking food to sell. She was also selling beer. It was so painful to stand such a noise almost every evening, but that was the only way auntie Therese could earn her living. The money she made was used for personal expenses like traveling to the State Capital where most of our relatives lived.

Every evening I would sit on my study—a

small table in the right corner of the living room to try to read, but not for too long. The customers would begin to come one by one to ask for my aunt. Some would be specific by asking if she had cooked. A "no" answer meant they would not come back. But a "yes" meant regardless of the time they would come again. A man I never knew had his voice "destroyed" by alcohol. When he spoke you thought he was going to run out of breath and die in the next few minutes. You know what I mean?

Even in the midst of those challenges I passed the "probatoire" exam. I failed the "Baccalauréat" on my first attempt before leaving Bafia.

The weather in Bafia is very hot. It would start getting warm in the morning till evening and I, who was visiting that part of the country after a very, very long period of absence, was in serious trouble. I could not stand the heat. When the sun was too hot it would make the aluminum roofs crack.

To go to school I would walk like many of my mates did. We could not afford taxi fares or get a ride from friends who were taxi drivers or benefit from the parent's or government financial help. I would walk the long distance that separated our house from the school under a very hot sunny day, walking on the tarred road.

That road was crowded with students who lived not very far from the campus. Others would spend noon at school. This was common and still happens in many schools of my country. Would you like to know what they ate at noon? No worry about that. Women would come and sell donut, beans and many other kind of food on campus. Apart from that, some students brought along their lunch. During the break, which was always at 10 o'clock they would eat half of that lunch and at noon they would eat the other half and stay until the end of the school day.

At the end of the class on Thursdays we would go to one of the famous market places in the town of Bafia. There were three actually, the "samba" market where buyers and sellers would come from remote areas of the town to sell and buy raw product like yams, cassava, plantains and many other different kind of vegetables from farmers. This market place was said to be the very first market place in town, because of its age.

The other market place, reputed for the selling of sugar cane was the "Market of Thursday" This market used to take place every Thursday. Sugar cane sellers would come from different villages in the peripherals of the town. We would see many students converge to the market sometimes just to walk around. They could sometimes buy some sugar. But most of them had friends who sold sugar canes and from whom they could expect to get some for free before going home. The market would close at 6pm, sometimes later. You would then see people holding a long sugar cane or even more than one in their hands while heading home.

Once at home they would proudly get someone's attention that they had been to the "Thursday's market". These were always signs of pride to show that someone had been to the market.

The biggest of all the markets of Bafia was "Ndjoumba." I do not know where that name came from, but to the best of my knowledge the market took its name from the fact that the people who were selling came from towns and cities other than Bafia. The other reason why I think that name was given is that the market is really big. So big that everything can be found there. People would come to "Ndjoumba" to sell and buy clothes. Others would come for food. As a matter of fact you could get your food cooked and made ready right on the spot. The market was situated far from the city center, but that would not prevent parents, students and visitors to turn up in a great number

The music coming from bars or some music stores or from someone's record player could be heard from a long distance. It was inside this noise combined with the voices of the crowd and sellers who would call customers and advertise their products that I found myself. They would shout to call mothers, students while holding an item in their hands. Sometimes they would hand the item to you as if they were giving it away. But it was a way to get you to buy it.

The whole scenario happens almost in every market place of my country, Cameroon. The expected result of the seller is to see his item purchased, and for the customer it is to get a good item at a cheap price. This ambiance was so attracting that every person wanted to go back to "Ndjoumba" the following week. "Ndjoumba" like the other market places was an open-air market place. Items are displayed on tables and on the floor.

I finally and successfully completed my studies in Bafia and had to leave now for the city capital Yaoundé, to prepare for college and the university.

At the State Capital

I had been to Yaoundé before, only as a visitor, on holidays. But this time I was there, as a student. I was not living very far from "Institut Victor Hugo". I could even walk to school. The means of transportation was personal cars, taxis and buses. Every morning from Monday to Friday I would wake up at around 6 am to start getting ready for school.

I first lived with my brother who had a girlfriend with kids. We shared a small one-bed room apartment. My brother would sleep in the bedroom with his girlfriend and the kids, while I would sleep in the living room, not on a nice and comfortable couch, but on a hard and cold-cemented floor, that I had previously covered with clothes and a few fabrics.

After a certain period of time my brother decided to move. I did not want to move with them, because they were already a big family and needed some space and I wanted to give them that. So I stayed at the same place alone.

Before living with them, I had lived with my uncle-in law, in a neighborhood called "Nsam Efoulan". As a matter of fact, when I graduated from High School, with the "Advanced Level", I was still living there. I was now qualified to go to university.

Even in Yaoundé I was still busy with the things of God. The church I was attending was located about 2 miles away from the house. And it took me some two hours to and fro. I walked because I could not afford transportation.

In the church I was mainly involved in the youth activities such as evangelism, singing and music with the church band. The youth held weekly, monthly and annual meetings where I took an active part. Some of the responsibility or duties that I carried out were: General Secretary of the chapel, and news director. Still in the church I was among the Sunday presiding officers either to lead the intercessory prayers or read the Sunday scriptures.

I was now a graduate from High School and was on the road to university as were many of my mates. But I faced some problems. The main problem was that I did not know what I was going to major in at the university. I had not been oriented. We were not given a formal orientation. I was advised to go and major in literature that I did love. But I would ask to myself "where would that take me in the end?" To be a journalist, a translator or an interpreter. I started having a clear idea of what I could be. I added more information to that and discovered that after three years at the university I would have to go to a training college. And that looked too long for me and costly and my parents could not afford that.

I was almost discouraged. I was really struggling with my mind and my future had almost narrowed. Then I had another idea: "Can't I go to a language center and learn English?" I did not really understand why I wanted to go to a language center. I did not want to be a teacher. But it was a relief to me after attempting and failing to complete training in Journalism at a private Advanced School of Mass Communication in 1994.

Look at what God did

I started learning English at the English Language Center, hosted by the British Council. Although I was among the best students and even got a registration for an International English Test, the FCE (First Certificate of English), I got stuck because of the lack of money. Despite that misfortune, I knew what I had to do even though I did not clearly understand it.

One day a friend of mine from church and I shared ideas on learning English and he suggested to me the "Bilingual Training Center". That was a learning center I had never heard about before. I later discovered that it was owned by the government and mainly staffed by Cameroonians. I rushed to the school and gathered all the necessary information and was enrolled as a student in an Upper Level.

I was determined to do whatever was necessary to succeed. I never missed a class. From that day I set myself a goal: To use every means at my disposal to pick up the English language. So I would be at the center sometimes out of my normal study hours. I would spend hours and hours in the Self Access Learning Center (SALC) reading, talking to people, doing lots and lots of personal work and research. I would sometimes help other students.

I remember one day a student of the center came up to me and asked me if I were a teacher. When I said, "no" he did not want to believe. For him my attitude and my skills showed that I was teaching at the center.

Some students after their class would look for me for more explanation on what they had done in the classroom. I had young people coming to me. Because they were planning to travel abroad, they needed to improve on their English. Most of them were traveling to England and the US to study. As you probably know, you need to have some Basic English knowledge and in some cases you must have taken one of the following exams: the TOEFL (Test

Of English as Foreign Language) or the CPE (Cambridge Proficiency Exam). I studied the materials and was able to explain what the exams were all about. I did not charge anything. But when the students insisted, I asked for a token fee and would not blame them if they could not give.

In a short period of time I became a kind of tutor or assistant teacher to a group of students from different levels in the center, to the point where I became popular, if not famous in the entire campus. If someone told you that I was a teacher, you would believe him or her at once. I had all the abilities and dispositions. Today the school still remembers that someone studied there and his name was David Moukon. My fame expanded so fast that I was invited to teach in homes and offices.

Through it all

That was not an easy task, because I did not have teaching experience. I had never attended a Teachers Training College. But what I believe I had was a special gift from God.

I taught around 15 people, among them an important businesswoman of the city capital, a National Assembly secretary. After a period of teaching of six months, she was able to help with translation on one of her trips to Germany. In fact she helped a passenger claim his luggage. When came back, she expressed her gratitude to me. I did not believe that she could achieve that much.

Another woman came to the center looking for me. She had heard from the lady who traveled to Germany, that there was a young man at the Yaoundé Pilot Linguistic Center who could help her speak English within six months, whether she had any previous English background or not.

She came to the center. I was absent. She left a message asking me to meet her in her office at a certain time, on a certain day. I met a woman of a strong personality and a kind heart. It was a loving woman in her 60s or so, but yet desiring to learn. After six months she was impressed by what she had accomplished and was able to say in English. In the midst of all that excitement she told me that she would open a school and I would be the English teacher. I could not believe my ears. God was showing me the way He wanted me to follow. That was not all that He wanted me to know and do. There was another desire in my heart: learning computer.

Instruments in God's hands for my favor

Now, watch this. Without even paying a single penny, I took my first computer course when I met a businessman named Bill. He wanted to improve on English and the two of us worked a deal. I would teach him English, and he would teach me computer. Deal? Deal. So he charged one of his workers to teach me computer from his consultant office and I was going to teach him English.

Still about the computer thing, there is an

organization in my country called the National Employment Fund (NEF). That organization helped me a lot and I must say here that I am grateful to its Director, Mr. Camille Mouthé à Bidias and the whole staff. Thanks to them I was able to complete training in Data Management at no cost, something I couldn't have done if I had to pay. It is at that same period that I started teaching at Sion-Ufrim, a school opened by Mrs. Sunjo Agnes, to whom I taught English previously. What an experience I am having in that anointed environment.

Mrs. Sunjo Agnes welcomed me in that place like her own son. She discovered the gifts of God that were in my life and knew that I was where God wanted me to be, before He could take me to the next level, for His glory.

I quite remember that I told to Mrs. Sunjio one day that I would write a book in which I would mention her name. Well, this is just the beginning of that promise being fulfilled. Having her name mentioned here is of a great significance, for the powerful and positive influence she had in my life cannot be fathomed.

A woman of love, a very attentive and detailed woman, who had no respect of person. She was kind and welcoming to everybody: children as well as adults. I met a woman of a strong will and a strong faith in God. A woman I will never forget. Mama Sunjio Agnès, you planted a seed in my heart.

That seed is growing perfectly. Thank you for your wisdom. May the richness of God fill your life through out all eternity.

God was at work and I was not aware of the fact that He was making a way for me to move to the United States of America. I could not believe that was happening to me.

When I was still studying English, even though I did not know why, the Spirit of the Lord told me that, the language would be used to study His Word and reach the world with the Gospel of Jesus Christ. Then I understood that God had put that gift in my life for His service. Finally I knew the purpose of God in my life. That was in 1997.

Three years later I watched God moving as He was preparing me to move out of my home country to the land He had promised. I knew that, but tried to move faster than God. I tried to make things happen on my own time and with my human limited abilities and power. But I failed. I had to wait upon the Lord. The Word of God says "He that waits upon the Lord shall renew his strength" and "the ways of the Lord are not our ways and His thoughts are not our thoughts."

Chapter Four
AN HUNGRY HEART FOR GOD

I was first baptized at the Presbyterian Church according to their doctrine at a very young age. My parents who are devoted Christians, very early showed me the way to church. Every Sunday I would go with other children of my age. We took very seriously the way we looked and our parents were also careful about that. We were clothed almost in the same attire every Sunday. The pants and the short sleeves shirt were of the same material and color matching with our shoes. When we were walking on the roadside on our way to church every eye was on us. With a smile on our faces and a sense of personality and holiness in our hearts we walked passing some young boys and girls of our ages, who had not "made it yet to heaven."

There were seats in the sanctuary reserved for children. But before entering the church for the Sunday service we had to attend the Sunday school in a room adjacent to the chapel. The lessons were mainly focusing on biblical stories, like the birth of Jesus, which was even performed by the children during Christmas. I still remember that I played the shepherd in one of those Christmas plays. Before that every child was taught to read the scriptures and memorize them. My favorite was John chapter one. I was given I think the first four verses to memorize before Christmas day. After Sunday school we would enter the House of God in line and silently. This silence was always observed not only in the church during sermons, but also in my heart.

My heart was filled with the desire to know Jesus more. When the youth ministry would hold their annual meeting called "the general conference" I would attend, not as an invited or official guest, but as a curious observer. The huge number of young men and women who came to the "general conference" fascinated me. I think I was 7 or 8 years old at that time. For me the age did not really matter. I looked around and was able to see some young boys, who were probably my age. I did not ask them, because I did not find myself worthy to approach those "angels of God." They were glooming with such a joy, displaying such a fellowship and communion that I had never seen before in my entire life.

The church officers had informed all the members about the event several months in advance and invited each one to pray and put aside some money and food as their own contribution to the "general conference". The assignment to make sure that all the provision was being gathered was given to the deacons of the church, to the elders and to the leaders of all the groups that made the church family. Some of them had the right to go from house to house to collect goods, especially when an old lady or a disable person was unable to take them to church, or send them by a church member. The simplicity, the devotion and liberality within which the preparation of the conference was flowing still amaze me. It was not a one man's event, but a family event and everybody was involved: young, old, visitors and sometimes-total strangers.

The conference planning was a grand mobilization for the members of the church, especially the youth who would be on the spotlight on that big day. I was mainly attracted by the dancing rehearsal in this entire scenario. At first I did not think that the dancing would be performed on that occasion. Generally the dancing groups performed when a dignitary would visit and the performance would not take place at church, as it was going to be the case at the conference, but at that dignitary's house. In addition to that the dancers would perform during the celebration marking the Youth Day (February 11th) and the Reunification Day (May 20th) in front of a big crowd.

The players used two drums and another traditional musical instrument made of iron. The dancers were young men and women dressed in a fabric tied around their waist, when they did not wear a traditional skirt made of "raffia" fibers. The men would leave their chest totally naked. But the women would cover up theirs. The dancers would follow the instructions of the leader, who most of the time was the best dancer or the oldest person in the group, because it was believed that they had a lot of experience.

The dancers would stand in line of two rows. One line was for men and another one for women and they would progress together exercising the same dancing step in perfect harmony with the body under the rhythm of the drums. The movement of the body was always impressive and executed with great majesty. The ladies would dance a lot by moving their breast, waist and back combined with a nice smile on their face, which would give to that presentation a total performance of great harmony and cultural picturing. The dancers would rehearse with no shoes on, and the practice would last for hours. I would be there until the end. I think that if I were asked to teach these dancing steps I would do it very well.

When I attended my first "general conference" as an observer two things caught my attention: the march and the lunch offered to the participants. They caught my attention because they were the most apparent and appealing too. I am certain that I would have searched for something more valuable than that, had I known the Lord and the importance of the Bible.

The participants were dressed in a white shirt and black pants for men and white shirt and black skirt for women. They would sing while marching along the sidewalk of the city's main road. Their voices would sound like a heavenly appeal from God to the population of Ntui. In a twinkling of an eye the road would be quickly invaded first by children, next by parents who would leave their businesses and homes to come and salute, by their presence along the road side, the passage of those children of God. While they were marching they would play their traditional musical instruments. We would follow those lines made in sections to church, where the welcome ceremonies were about to begin.

These ceremonies were made to welcome the delegations, and were combined with dances. Each delegation present came from a town far away from Ntui and each one belonged to a parish that they came to represent at the event. We had for example the following parishes represented: Baliama, Boulaga, Ngoro, Tiekani, Donenkeng, Goura and of course Ntui, just to name these few.

Every delegation had a leader, who would either be the president of the youth group, the youth coordinator, a chaplain, one of the church elders, or simply their pastor. The pastors were so lovely and fun to be with. A picture just came in my mind of one of them, who actually took part in the race and the soccer games with the youth. That humbles me till this day.

The introduction of the delegation was very

simple. When they called the name of the parish, the participants representing the parish would stand up clapping their hands and singing. And while they sang some of them would execute some dance steps. They had prepared a song for that particular moment and the message behind it was "we are greeting you." The song that was sung in one of our dialects moved people to sing, dance and clap their hands. I knew about all this, when a few years later I joined the movement.

The dancing ceremony would take place in front of some local church leaders and village authorities: elders, pastors, priests, mayors...etc. The performance would raise a lot of money for the dancers. It must be mentioned that the dancers were not dancing to be paid or rewarded. If that was the case, they could have gathered the coins and notes that people came to drop in a small basket placed just on the side of the church front yard.

When it was time for lunch I would stand out of the refectory, a giant tent made of palm tree branches and pools, as the participants ate. I would sometimes enter in if someone called me. What I admired most once inside was the spirit of fraternity, joy and unity that prevailed. As I was watching and thinking, I knew I was missing something. My heart was thirsty of the desire to become a part of such a group and I had been looking for ways to experience these gifts too.

My admiration for the youth movement kept growing day after day. And when I got to middle school, in grade 8, to be exact, my heart began to be opened up more and more to the things of God. I began to spend time in prayer, worship and constant Bible reading and Scriptures meditation. Christian songs attracted me so much so that I could recognize one from a distance. I thought one day that everybody was hearing what I was hearing. But they were not. One day as we were coming back from school I told to my teacher, "Can you hear that Christian song? He said 'no' whereas I was hearing it."

My "new birth"

At the age of 17 I accepted Jesus Christ in my life. At that same moment I was allowed to partake of the Lord's Supper. Certain requirements had to be met to partake as the doctrine of the church I was brought in stated.

The preparation for this important day of my life started with a written exam we had to take. We were given a set of Bible questions and also questions related to the doctrine of the church. All those questions were contained in a book called catechism.

It took me a few weeks to learn the catechism. Neither my parents nor my brothers and sister knew that I was going to write that exam in preparation of my consecration, despite the fact that they would see me reading the document frequently at home.

I sat for the exam and passed. I was the

second best student who scored the highest grade. I informed my parents about the Holy Communion Day. They could not provide food, clothing and invite guests, because they did not have money. But my elder brother went to the market that day and bought me a brown shirt. I did not like it, because of its dark color. I wanted something more radiant. My brother went back to the market and brought another shirt. The color was sky blue with some vertical stripes. I liked that one better. I remember that, that day my dad got mad at me and said: "Don't be too demanding".

On December 25th 1988, I was standing before God and many witnesses to publicly confess Jesus Christ as Lord and Savior of my life. The church service that day was different. There was a new item on the agenda. Therefore the service would be longer than usual.

The church members were aware of the fact that they would stay in service longer than it had always been. So many of them would eat very well at home and make provision for their babies.

When the pastor finished making some additions to the announcement he informed the folks that he would proceed with the baptism and the Holy Communion sacraments. Then he invited us to stand to the front and face the altar.

Although the church was full to capacity the deacons managed to reserve the first seats for us, whose entrance into the kingdom of God was happening that day. As you know during ordinary church services, in almost every assembly of the world you won't see as many people as you see on Christmas and Easter services. Am I not correct? We would number for instance 170 people during ordinary Sundays, but during the two major Christians celebrations, you would probably number the double of that figure.

Knowing what would always happen on those circumstances, the "elect" would be asked to come early on Sunday and occupy the front seats on pews. In the church people sat in three long pews on benches according to the group or associations they may belong to in the congregation.

The men's and youth's associations would sit in the same pew at the same row on the right, whereas the middle pews were reserved for children, mothers with children and "the elects". The third pews were to be occupied by the women association and elders.

On the first pew there was a choir group essentially composed of men. Most of the songs that they sang were in French or "Bafia"-my mother tongue. Still, in that pew a seat would be offered to a visitor or an official who had chosen to visit that day.

The middle pews were occupied by the people who would take the Holy Communion and those who would be baptized. The last pew had its choir group like in the first pews. If in the first pew you would find mainly men, here there would be mainly women. All these pews would face the altar. The church elders were seating on the left of the altar, whereas the seats on the right were reserved for the members of the church band, which I would be a part of later.

The pastor invited us to stand up and walk forward each one with his spiritual father. I suddenly realized that I did not have one, and then I turned to my mother to ask her who my spiritual father was. And sadly she whispered to me, that he'd passed away. I almost cried. A well-known man and dedicated Christian, who noticed our embarrassment walked straight and quickly and stood behind me, like every other spiritual father, before the pastor could even reach me. I felt a great relief.

As it is usually the case during such ceremonies, you have to answer some questions as a confession before men and God that you believe that Jesus Christ is your Lord and Savior from that day. About five questions were asked of us and we replied by raising our right hand followed by "yes I believe." I believed that day that Jesus was my Lord and Savior. The handshake of the pastor came to put me in total confidence with God's promise through the Holy Spirit. Songs of glory to God were sung when the band did not play after the prayer of one of the elders, most of the time the one who followed the pastor during the ceremonies. Something new happened to me that day.

The celebration

As you probably know, when you have joy you want to share it. You want to share it not only with your family and your brethren, but also with your friends. I could not enjoy my salvation that way and I was not even thinking of that because my family did not have money to afford a salvation party. But surprisingly a neighbor's son had organized a party to which he invited many of his friends. They had started when he was informed that I had given my life to the Lord. The party, which did not have a real purpose before, was now turned into the celebration of my "new birth". Praise the Lord.

My life was really changed from that day forward. I became a child of God. I was regenerated and started to sense and experience the presence of God in my life every day. I was no more going out at night, in the clubs with friends or hanging out with girls, stealing or lying. I was delivered from those bondages and started walking in the light of God, until this day.

The Holy Spirit was constantly talking to me. I was born again. My life was truly changed. My new life became a life of prayers, the reading of the Scriptures, meditation, and prayer meetings, counseling of youth, leadership in the youth's ministry, serious implication and involvement in the things of God. This last element was very important to me.

"I must be by my Father's business"

The first time I was invited to preach is one of the memorable day of my life. I still remember that I preached from Luke 12:13-21. This passage is followed by the story of the foolish rich man, all of them taken from the New Testament. The feedback was unexpected.

Many church members came to congratulate me. Some even began to say: "You will be a pastor some day." Soon the pastor would send me with some deacons and elders of the church to go and evangelize in some remote areas of the city. Evangelism was a new notion to me, but the excitement and privilege that I felt motivated me so much. I never asked any question to my team members like, "what are we going to talk about or who is going to say what?" They all knew that I was going to be the preacher.

The very first village I ever went to was called Nguété. I preached in the house of the chief of the village. He was not really the chief, but a well-known man who joyfully opened his house to welcome our team. The team was made of three people if I am not mistaken and I was the youngest, but yet on fire for the Lord.

My message came from the story of John the Baptist preaching in the wilderness in Luke 3:3-17. After this message and as we were about to leave, that man (chief) went into his room and came out with a suit, handed it to me and said: "This is for your message on John the Baptist." The name of that man was Jean Bonda. I witnessed the blessing of God that day and that blessing has been following me all the days of my life. "Surely goodness and mercy shall follow me all the days of my life..." Psalm 23:6

In the church band I would sing and play the lead guitar; in the youth ministry I would preach and pray, in the prayer meetings in homes I would preside, and pray; in the leadership and many other works the Lord would invite me to, His anointing was always present with me and in me, spreading all around me, even crossing the borders.

As a matter of fact a report on me even reached some of my relatives who lived on the other side of town. I remember that one of them came to pay a visit to my family. At lunch he told me," I hear that when you sing, people kneel down to pray." Praise God. Well, I never noticed that and I never even prepared for that. People kept telling things that I did, but I did not even remember. It was not only the singing; it was also the preaching and the dedication to the work of God. Because of it I never took a rest. I was constantly at my pastor's feet to learn the things of God and help him in his visits and prayers. Because of my regular presence at the presbytery, some parishioners began calling me, "the child of the pastor."

At school as well as at home people would

call me pastor, because I would spend most my time talking about God. I was among the best students in catechism class (Bible Study class) although I was not among the best in general. I still remember that I won a prize in middle school before leaving my town. That prize was a reward for my good performance in Bible Study. My pastor, Rev. Ngon Emmanuel, presented it to me; I owe him all my gratitude too. He helped me, and mentored me. He was a father to me. Would you like me to tell you what the prize was? It was my very first copy of the New Testament. I was truly filled with joy, for being so blessed. And another one was coming. I passed the GCE "O" Level. That was the General Certificate of Education Ordinary Level, which opened me the doors to High School. I passed it after spending many years living with my parents under a "tyrannical" father's dictatorship system and a caring mother.

Chapter Five
ETERNAL SECURITY: THE REVELATION
As I stated before, I gave my life to Jesus Christ, when I was 17. But at the age of 21 many thoughts and provoking questions started haunting my mind, especially on the theme of salvation. I rejected the truth that we were saved. I quite remember that a high school friend and I entered an argument on that theme. Of course I was wrong, but I did not know and did not even want to try the scriptures.

At the age of 30 the Lord, through the booklet **_"Have you heard of the four spiritual laws?"_** was going to reveal Himself to me. I read this booklet a few months before, but its content was still superficial to me. All that I received by reading it was simply intellectual knowledge. The Spirit of God had not truly awakened me yet to the reality of the person of Christ. I trusted in Him. I knew Him, but not in a personal and intimate way. Although I was saved, I debated a lot and the reality of Christ still escaped me.

On September 2nd 2001, one day after my birthday the Lord drew my attention to His Word and kept me motionless before it. My thirtieth birthday was that Saturday, September 1st 2001. I was cleaning the house that day, when my prayer partner Antoine Kayoka came to the house and offered me a birthday gift. It was a small book in French entitled: Comment faire connaître Jesus-Christ, "how to make Jesus Christ known", by late Dr. Bill Bright.

Bill And Vonette Bright

"Bill and Vonette Bright are founders of Campus Crusade for Christ, International. In 1951, Bill and Vonette Bright pursued their passion for ministry by starting Campus Crusade for Christ at the University of California at Los Angeles.

What began with college students has since grown into one of the largest international Christian ministries in the world, reaching beyond students to serve inner cities, the military, athletes, political and business leaders, the entertainment industry, and families.

The Brights spent more than half a century building and leading Campus Crusade for Christ to its current size of more than 27,000 staff members and 225,000 volunteers working in 190 countries.

However, their influence has reached far beyond the ministry of Campus Crusade for Christ."

Bill Bright

"Bill's unique blend of Christian commitment and communications insight was at the heart of his success.

His *Four Spiritual Laws booklet*—a 4-point outline written by Bill in 1956 on how to establish a personal relationship with Jesus—has been printed in some 200 languages.

Although religious tracts have been published for centuries, Bill's booklet has become what is considered to be the most widely disseminated religious booklet in history, with more than 2.5 billion booklets distributed to date.

Bill was considered a major catalyst for the modern-day resurgence of the disciplines of fasting and prayer in the Christian church.

In 1996, Bill was presented with the prestigious Templeton Prize for Progress in Religion, for his work with <u>fasting and prayer</u>. Worth more than $1 million, the Templeton Prize is the world's largest financial annual award. Bill donated all of his prize money to causes promoting the spiritual benefits of fasting and prayer.

Bill also co-founded, with Dr. James Davis, the Global Pastors Network, an Internet-based training center, designed to equip pastors and ministers worldwide with interactive resources, events, and networking opportunities.

Bill Bright died in 2003, from complications related to pulmonary fibrosis, at the age of 81." "…He being dead yet speaketh" (Hebrews 11:4). God spoke to me through the *Four Spiritual Laws*.

The Four Spiritual Laws

Dear reader what I am about to share with you is what totally changed my life and it is with an eager heart, that I invite you to follow carefully these principles that might be the beginning a life changing experience for you.

Do you have an idea what it might take to begin a relationship with God? Do you think by devoting yourself to unselfish religious deeds, maybe? Or do you think that by becoming a better person God will accept you?

You may be surprised that none of those things will work. But God has made it very clear in the Bible how we can know Him.

Law 1:

God loves you and offers a wonderful plan for your life.

God's Love

"For God so loved the world, that He gave His only begotten Son, that whosoever believeth in Him should not perish, but have everlasting life." (John 3:16)

God's Plan

[Christ speaking] " I am come that they might have life, and that they might have it more abundantly" (John 10:10)

Why is it that most people are not experiencing the abundant life?

Because...

Law 2:

All of us sin and our sin has separated us from God.

We Are Sinful

"For all have sinned, and come short of the glory of God" (Romans 3:23)

We were created to have fellowship with God; but, because of our stubborn self-will, we chose to go our own independent way, and fellowship with God was broken. This self-will, characterized by an attitude of active rebellion or passive indifference, is evidence of what the Bible calls sin.

We Are Separated

"For the wages of sin is death" [spiritual separation from God].

This diagram illustrates that God is holy and people are sinful. A great gulf separates us. The arrows illustrate that we are continually trying to reach God and the abundant  life through our own efforts, such as a good life, philosophy, or religion—but we inevitably fail.

The third law explains the only way to bridge this gulf...

Law 3:

Jesus Christ is God's only provision for our sin. Through Him we can know and experience God's love and plan for our life.

He died in Our Place

"But God commandeth His love toward us, in that, while we were yet sinners, Christ died for us." (Romans 5:8)

He Rose From the Dead

"Christ died for our sins according to the scriptures...He was buried...He rose again the third day...He was seen of Cephas, then of the twelve...He was seen of above five hundred brethren at once..." (1 Corinthians 15:3-5)

He Is the Only Way to God

"Jesus saith unto him, I am the way, the truth, and the life: no man cometh to the father, but by me." (John 14:6)

This diagram illustrates that God has bridged the gulf, which separates us from Him by sending His Son, Jesus Christ, to die on the cross in our place to pay the penalty for our sins.

It is not enough just to *know these three laws...*

Law 4:

<u>We must individually receive Jesus Christ as Savior and Lord; then we can know and experience God's love and plan for our lives.</u>

We Must Receive Christ

" But as many as receiveth Him, to them gave He power to become the sons of God, even to them that believe on his name." (John 1:12)

We Receive Christ Through Faith

" For by grace are ye saved through faith; and that not of yourselves: it is the gift of God: Not of works, lest any man should boast." (Ephesians 2:8-9)

When We Receive Christ, We Experience a New Birth

We Receive Christ By Personal Invitation

[Christ speaking] " Behold, I stand at the

door, and knock: if any man hear my voice, and open the door, I will come in to him, and will sup with him, and he with me." (Revelation 3:20)

Receiving Christ involves turning to God from self (repentance) and trusting Christ to come into our lives to forgive our sins and to make us what He wants us to be. Just to agree intellectually that Jesus Christ is the Son of God and that He died on the cross for your sins is not enough. Nor is it enough to have an emotional experience. You receive Jesus Christ by faith, as an act of the will.

These two circles represent two kinds of lives:

Self-Directed Life

Self is on the throne, directing decisions and actions (represented by the dots), often resulting in frustration. Jesus is outside the life.

Christ-Directed Life

Jesus is in the life and on the throne. Self is yielding to Jesus. The person sees Jesus' influence and direction in their life.

Which circle best describes your life?

Which circle would you like to have represent your life?

The following explains how you can receive Christ:

You can receive Christ right now by faith through prayer

Prayer is talking to God. God knows your heart and is not so concerned with your words as He is with the attitude of your heart. The following is a suggested prayer:

" Lord Jesus, I need You. Thank You for dying on the cross for my sins. I open the door of my life and receive You as my Savior and Lord. Thank You for forgiving my sins and giving me eternal life. Take control of the throne of my life. Make me the kind of person You want me to be"

If this prayer expresses the desire of your heart, then you can pray this prayer right now and Christ will come into your life, as He promised.

Does this prayer express the desire of your heart? Pray it now and Jesus will come into your heart.

I read the book all night long. That book explained the "Four Spiritual Laws". While I was reading my focus was on how to present the content to someone else. What I didn't know was that the Lord was getting ready to meet me right where I was in a supernatural way for the beginning of a life changing experience.

It was already midnight when I had a burning desire to look for the brochure "Have you heard of The Four Spiritual Laws?" But I postponed the search and went to bed.

The next morning was Sunday. After my morning prayer I began looking for the "Four

Spiritual Laws". I finally found the dusty and almost torn "treasure" hidden inside a drawer. Before that I had read again the book my partner offered me and there was a prayer inside. I said the prayer. It goes like this: ***"Lord Jesus, thank you for your love. Thank you that by your death and resurrection my sins were forgiven and that I can live a victorious and fruitful life everyday for you. In order to express my love to you and every man and in obedience to your commandments, I would like to give priority to preach the Gospel around me. Thanks for your promise to fructify me in your service. Amen"***

I just felt such a relief after finding the booklet. I thanked God for that and laid the booklet on my desk, so that I might not forget to take it when leaving for church.

I prayed God to touch the hearts of the people He wanted me to share the Word with.

I was already late for the Sunday service while I was getting ready. I just finished pressing my clothes and needed now to take a shower. But spontaneously, as I was trying to enter the bathroom my hand was drawn by a supernatural power to the table where the booklet was laying and I picked it up and began to read aloud, after I had turned the radio off.

My aim, by reading this booklet aloud was to practice how to present the Word of God to people.

Therefore I was reading and acting at the same time as if someone was right in front of me, listening to me. I was speaking as if I was presenting Jesus Christ to a listener; I was doing my best to persuade. With conviction and energy in my voice, "I was sharing Christ."

I finished reading the three first laws and totally agreed with what the Lord was saying.

I reached the fourth law. I said the prayer that followed and moved to the next page. I was first of all going to read this: *The Bible promises eternal life to everyone who receives Jesus Christ.* The next Scripture was the one that really got my attention the most.

It went like this: ***"And this is the record that God hath given to us eternal life, and this life is in his Son. He that hath the Son hath life; and he that hath not the Son of God hath not life. These things have I written unto you that believe on the name of the Son of God; that ye may know that ye have eternal life, and that ye may believe on the name of the Son of God.*** (*1 John 5:11-13)*

After reading that, I was motionless and speechless. I was unable to turn to the next page. I could not read the rest of the booklet. I walked to the door, which was closed. I could not say a single word. I did not understand what was happening to me. I spoke to God and said, "Father, are you saying that, since I accepted Jesus Christ, I have eternal life?

The response that hit my spirit was spontaneous and powerful, "yes". I jumped on my feet, ran into the bathroom, singing with joy while taking my shower. Something unusual happened to me that day.

Before leaving the house that Sunday morning I prayed to God that I might testify of what He had done in my life. I asked Him to help me share the "Four Spiritual Laws" with people whose hearts He had already touched. Maybe you felt the same way the day you encountered Jesus Christ. I could not get over the burning desire to make Jesus known to anyone I could meet. All I wanted to do was to share Christ. I wanted people to know about what had happened to me. I now understand best John 4 about the Samaritan woman.

I was late for church that day. That was not common to me. The choir was already in line for the Sunday procession. They asked me to go and put on my gown, but there was none left. I entered the sanctuary. Five minutes later the Sunday school leader invited me to lead some hymns with the congregation while the procession was coming in.

I Could Not Hold Myself Back

After the service I quickly left the sanctuary to meet a man I had promised to talk to when we where in the taxi. But I did not see him. I almost got cold and discouraged. But I knew the Holy Spirit was there to reassure me.

In the crowd the Lord sent me to a young

67

man. I greeted him and asked him how he found the Sunday message. I also asked him if the message had added anything to his relationship with Jesus Christ. And finally I asked him if he had ever heard of the "Four Spiritual Laws". As an answer to that last question, he said, "no". So I took him to a corner and began to share the brochure with him. From time to time he was going to turn his head away, but the Lord led me to say, "Look". So every time I used that word he would regain focus.

While we were talking, another young man, who was first listening in a distance, came closer. We were already reading the fourth law. I said the prayer first alone and I asked to both of them, if that prayer expressed the desire of their hearts. They said, "Yes" and I asked them to say the prayer themselves. They invited Jesus Christ in their lives right there. To close we prayed again together before they left.

Before the end of the day four people gave their lives to Jesus.

Chapter Six
"HE THAT WINS SOULS..."

"The fruit of righteous is a tree of life; and he that winneth souls is wise"

Proverbs11: 30

On Monday, September 3rd 2001 I asked the Lord to put on my path people who would give Him their lives. I was late to work that day. When I got there, I saw a man standing at the main entrance of our office. That was my dad. I was not informed, that my dad would visit me. What generally occasions the visit of a relative to the city is the announcement of an event like a wedding ceremony of a family member or a job promotion. Beside joyful events, the family gathers also during bereavements. It is usually an opportunity to see uncles, aunts and cousins that we have not seen for years and an occasion to meet some we never knew were part of the family. None of the above suggestions were the motives of my dad's trip to the Nation's Capital, but certainly a divine appointment was.

As I was taking the stairs to go to my office, I told to my co-worker, "I have received the assurance of eternal life." She said: "David, I don't understand." I promised to talk to her about it later. Her name is Mary. She worked at the reception and was in charge of many other office duties like making photocopies, binding books, managing the phone booth and of course welcoming customers with her God-given smile. She was not the only co-worker I had. To the best of my knowledge I had approximately five. That number increased with the birth of the professional training school I will talk more about soon. In the meantime I was going to meet my visitor.

My father and I started to talk. And I told him that I had received the assurance of eternal life in the name of Jesus Christ. I shared my testimony with him. My dad was listening to me very carefully. And he made a confession to me. He had never made any to anybody in the family. He told me why he had stopped going to church. It was because what people preached was never what they did. He himself added that we should not follow men, but God. He promised me that day to start going back to church again and partake in the Lord Supper as before. While I was talking to my dad, an uncle walked in. And just a few minutes after, a cousin walked in. My dad left to go and greet my other brothers who lived in the city. Meanwhile my uncle was at the door ready to leave. I saw both of them off and I went to meet my cousin.

We started to talk about social life when I told him, that something had happened to me and that I wanted to share it with him. We shared the "*Four Spiritual Laws*." He accepted Christ. He promised me to come back two days later. He gave me his phone number. I gave him a warm handshake before he left. Him and I had been attending church since our early age, but I had never shared my Christian experience with him. I never thought I would one day. Not that I couldn't, but just because I had "no life" to share. The look on his face when he said he was going to come back again spoke a genuine eagerness to know Jesus Christ more. I promised to give him a copy of the *"Four Spiritual Laws"* on his next visit. Unfortunately I was off that day and couldn't show up at work. He was kind of upset and said, "How can you stop when you have started giving something sweet to somebody?" For him, the Good News I shared with him was sweet and the booklet would help him to keep enjoying that sweetness. I believe the Holy Spirit kept the sweetness of the Word of God in his heart.

Still on the same day, my students had decided to offer a party on my birthday celebration. That was a great surprise for me. But before the party began, I shared the "*Four Spiritual Laws*" with a co-worker who accepted Jesus Christ. He was not attending a church. I read Hebrews 10:25 to him. It reads, "Not forsaking the assembling of yourselves together, as the manner of some is; but exhorting one another: and so much the more, as ye see the day approaching." After those words he promised, that he would start looking for a church. When you start looking for a church, do it prayerfully and God will lead you to a Bible-believing church where Jesus Christ is exalted and the Scripture taught with categories.

During my birthday party, the students asked me to say a word. I said that, "We all need to personally invite Jesus Christ in our lives." At the end of my testimony I saw a bright smile on one of my friends' faces. I sensed in my spirit that they had been touched by the power of God, and the radiant smile was the external visualization of what the Holy Spirit was doing on the inside. While we were sharing the cake, two ladies had been waiting for me downstairs. I left my students and went to meet the two ladies.

One of them told me that she had a lot of problems and I replied that, Jesus Christ was the solution to her problems, and I proceeded by telling her that Jesus had done something wonderful in my life. She gave me her attention. I asked her if she'd ever heard about the "*Four Spiritual Laws.*" She said, "No". I presented them to her and she accepted Christ in her life. I encouraged her to join a Bible believing church. I had been insisting on being a part of a Christian family or a Christian congregation where Jesus Christ is worshiped and the truth of the Bible taught, because Jesus Christ has a Body and that Body is made of every single person who has accepted Him in their lives, to display His nature and character in a lost and dying world.

It was 2pm and I needed to go home. But the Father wanted me to stay a little bit longer. Suddenly I saw another cousin coming--a police officer--. We shared the leftover birthday cake, before I began telling him that my life had been changed and I proposed to show him how. I shared the "Four Spiritual Laws" with him. He accepted Jesus. Something that I noticed with him was that he read each line of the suggested prayer twice. I encouraged my cousin to read the Bible every day, pray to God always and have fellowship with other believers. I finally encouraged him to join a Bible believing church where Jesus Christ was worshipped. After our closing prayer I looked at the countenance of his face. It was radiant. I watched him walk out. I knew something had taken place in his life. I knew he was a new man, a transformed man.

My friend, giving your life to Jesus Christ is a wonderful thing. It is a personal decision. You don't receive Jesus Christ from birth and no one can make that decision in your place. It is a thoughtful, willing and personal decision that you make. Personal? Yes personal. Your grandfather, father and mother or grandmother positions in the church does not make you a born again Christian. You are still lost and fallen from the glory of God. But when you personally accept Christ, believe that you have eternal life. I did not have that assurance, although I knew who Jesus Christ was. I hope you will stop being an activist like I was. Stop that "show" now and be real, honest and admit your failures. Ask Jesus Christ, by faith to come into your life and He will come just as He promised

The Lord was not through me yet. My dad was going to spend the night with me. He was so tired that he went to bed early that Monday night of 2001. Before going to bed I spent some time in prayer and Bible reading, as I usually did not expecting God's visitation on the following day.

On Tuesday morning he was the first to get up. And he went back to lie down. I still wanted to sleep. A power I could not control began to open my eyes. I tried to resist, but I could not. Then a voice spoke to me saying, "Invite your dad for prayer." "What? He is still sleeping. I am not going to disturb him. This is my dad. I can't do that." The Spirit of God told me, "Don't you remember what I have done for you." Right there, with my eyes wide opened, I looked at my dad. He was not even sleeping as I thought. With a calm, but firm voice I said, "We're going to pray, dad." "Ok", he replied. I couldn't believe that. Was it real what I was seeing, that I was calling my dad to pray? Thirty years after I was born, that was the major invitation I had ever given to my father. He humbly accepted it.

We sat down. After the prayer I showed him the "*Four Spiritual Laws*". I also explained how many lives had been changed by its message. I proposed to share its content with him. He agreed. I learnt in soul winning to always have your "weapons" ready. The booklet was not hidden somewhere and the information that I gave him regarding the impact its message had had in many lives around the world was not an invention. Actually I could show to my dad where everything I was telling him was found. The Bible is my best reference book. How about you?

It was 6 o'clock in the morning. Here I was sitting so close than I had ever been to my dad, presenting the Gospel of Jesus Christ to him. He was listening to me carefully. He was nodding every time I read. The profound quietness and silence of my dad had always been a big concern to me. He never spoke a lot, but it never meant, that he agreed with everything you said, even when he nodded his head.

We finished reading the three first laws. We were now reading the fourth. When I began to read it, the tune of my voice started to change. The enemy was trying to put doubt and confusion in me, but the Holy Spirit helped me and we reached the promise of Revelation 3:20. My dad laughed after we read that promise. This is another thing you need to know about my dad. He smiles and laughs at everything that is funny even when you know you are delivering a serious address. The knock on the door and Jesus coming to sup with you was funny for my dad, because he heard it literally. I had to interpret that before he could well understand. I began to ask my dad questions about the images on the booklet, about the self-centered life and the Christ-centered life. He answered so well. But I helped him to know that he could receive Jesus Christ in his life by inviting Him.

I said the suggested prayer. There was such serenity over my dad while I was reading it. As soon as I had finished, I asked to my dad if that prayer expressed the desire of his heart. "Yes", he calmly said. Then I asked him to say the prayer himself.

It was not easy, because his hands were shaking when he was trying to hold the booklet. He could read, but you had to make sure that the letters were big enough. All this was the result of my dad's age and the impact of the hard work he performed, that always required physical strength. I helped my dad to pray, and accept Jesus Christ. He prayed again to thank God for what He had done in his life. At the end we prayed together. And he told me that; he had seen that booklet in our house, in the village. To close we sang a hymn that my dad knew very well.

Before leaving that day, I noticed that my dad had picked up another booklet from my desk. That booklet was entitled "L'Appel", "The Calling". God might had been calling my to an assignment that I did not know. But from the biblical prospective, I believe that Jesus was calling my dad to follow Him, so that He might make him a "fisher of man." As soon as the Samaritan got saved she went straight to tell to a whole village what Jesus had done for her. After his close encounter with Jesus Christ on the road of Damascus Paul immediately started to preach the Good News to the Gentiles. When I got saved and received the assurance of salvation through Christ by revelation I wanted everybody to hear the Message. How about you, have told to somebody that Jesus saved you? If I did not tell to my dad, he would not be saved.

He was filled with joy when we were leaving the house. I could see it. I overhead him telling to a friend: "I am glad I made this trip to the city." We were standing at the roadside that day, as he was now preparing to go back to the village. What was designed to be a simple visit turned to be the homecoming celebration of the "prodigal son."

I continued to share my testimonies. I wrote it down and shared with some ministries of the Campus Crusade for Christ International from the French speaking countries. I went to Christian bookstores to drop some copies of my testimony for the edifying of the Body. Every time I had an opportunity to share Christ I would do so by talking about what He did in my life. I did so during one of the youth retreat. I shared the "Four Spiritual Laws" with about fifteen of them. I went on doing it for two days and 9 people accepted Christ. To God be the glory.

Before coming to America, I shared my testimony with around 30 people who committed their lives to Jesus Christ. God did it. No man comes to God except God Himself draws Him. He did the drawing and I only made myself available and willing. For so long I cried to be used by God, but I always thought, that I had to be a pastor first. That's wrong and I want you to know that the Great Commission is a call to every single believer, who is genuinely born again.

Go ye therefore, and teach all nations, baptizing them in the name of the Father, and of the Son, and of the Holy Ghost: Matthew 28:19

Teaching them to observe all things whatsoever I have commanded you: and, lo, I am with you alway, even unto the end of the world. Amen. Matthew 28:20

And this is the record that God hath given us eternal life, and this life is in his Son. He that hath the Son hath life; and he that hath not the Son of God hath not life. These things have I written unto you that believe on the name of the Son of God; that ye may know that ye have eternal life, and that ye may believe on the name of the Son of God. 1 John 5:11-13

YOU CAN BE SAVED

Jesus Christ loves and cares for you. To demonstrate His love for you God gave Him to the world so that through Him [Jesus] you might be saved from your sins. The Bible says: **"For God so loved the world that He gave His only begotten Son that whosoever believeth in Him should no perish but have everlasting life –** *John 3:16.*

Jesus came so that we might have life and that we might have it more abundantly [life with meaning and purpose]—*John 10:10.*

Not everybody experiences the abundant life the Bible talks about, because of sin. Sin separates man from God. "For all have sinned and come short of the glory of God," *Romans 3:23.*

Jesus Christ alone is the only answer to the problem of sin and the separation of man from God.

By an act of trust in Him you can be forgiven and experience the abundant life of John 10:10. Simply pray: ***"Lord Jesus, I need you. I open the door of my heart and receive you as Savior and Lord. Forgive all my sins. Amen."***

If you said this prayer you are now a child of God, born from above into the family of God. Join a Bible believing church, read the Bible constantly (starting with the Gospel of John), talk to God through prayer and tell someone what God has done for you.

Chapter Seven
GOODBYE CAMEROON, HELLO AMERICA

"Hello brother", "Yes". "This is Brother Emmanuel, how are you doing?" "I am fine, thank you." "You said you were looking for a job?" "Yes." "Is that all you want to do?" "Well, If I could work and go to school, that would be fine." "What do you want to go to school for?" "To study the Word of God. To study the Bible." "Do you think that's where God wants you to go?" "Yes". Those were the first words I exchanged with Brother Emmanuel that morning of a day I will never forget.

Emmanuel Leonard had been living in the United States for a long time. The first time we met was in a school where we went to work as volunteers. Emmanuel is a man of God as the two other men, who accompanied him that day. He is a very simple man, spontaneous. He is straightforward. He loves talking to people. Emmanuel always wants to make sure you are doing well.

Before leaving the school that day we said goodbye to each other. It was at that moment that I was introduced, not as a young man coming from Cameroon, Africa, as it was the case when I greeted the men earlier. I was now introduced as a gentleman who was looking for a job. "What type of job are you looking for", someone asked me. "A computer related job", I replied. "I was a computer analyst," I added. And I concluded that, I studied data management. Emmanuel had taken note of all the information, before we left to head home that Saturday evening.

Although I was tired, I was happy that I gained some experience working as a volunteer in an American elementary school. It was a privilege for me.

It was a wide building located far from the main road. From outside you could not know that there were nice equipments inside.

We entered through the door made of glass and were welcome by a nice lady. Right inside you could see a long corridor in front of you and others on the left and right of the building. We walked for a while on the long corridor where we saw a big hall on the left.

In the hall, there were books well arranged in shelves. There were also computers, desks and chairs. On the wall, there were book advertisements and instructions from the school administration to library users. After "signing in our names". You had to get used to that expression-sign in your name-almost everywhere you would go.

So, after that my brother Hamilton told me that the library we were in was for elementary school students. "What?" I exclaimed. "With such equipment," I added. "If this library was built back in my home country it would be offered to university students. "This is for elementary students," he insisted. The globe that had been placed on the table at the corner caught our attention as we were walking around. So, we stood to have a look. That was an opportunity for me to show to some friends where I was coming from.

It was September 2001

God opened the doors of America to me on 9/30/01 at 6:30 pm.

It was on Saturday after my family had seen me off at the Nsimalem International Airport that I left my country (Cameroon) for America. The great America was a new country to me. A country I heard about, read about and even dreamt about several years before. A country I had never been to before. This is a country the whole world watches. Many had been dreaming to go to America. It is "The promised land" to some and to others the land that "flows with milk and honey."

I had never flown a plane before. I was taken to the Customer Service by a relative at the Airport in Yaoundé. My relative apparently knew what I had to do. They had to check my luggage, my ticket before checking my passport and visa. After all that was done I spent some time with my family in the lobby. They all were confident, that I was going to have nice and safe trip to the US by the grace of God and encouraged me to pray and serve God as He had called me to.

The waiting room was not so crowded. We were all sitting waiting for the departure time Once more our passport and flight tickets as well as our belongings were checked. We held them while entering the plane.

While waiting to get on I opened my New Testament and started reading the Psalm. I was constantly talking to God, telling Him that I was going to America to do His Will.

It was time to enter the plane. As we were entering I hardly realized that we were walking through a hallway or sort of tunnel. I thought that my family would actually see me getting on the steps of the plane and that they could wave at me and me to them, just like the president of the Republic does when he leaves the country or comes back from a visit overseas. My case was different. I even thought that I could have had some pictures taken by a friend. We had started taking some and were immediately stopped by a security guard.

On the plane each of us was sitting on the seat assigned to them according to the seat number they were given. When I found my seat with the help of an airhostess, I sat. I did not know how to fasten my belt. I asked to a lady at the other seat on my right. She did not know either. Together we tried and finally succeeded. The announcement came as we were sitting in that big flying "bird" that was about to take off and meet the air.

I was amazed all the time at what was happening. It was like a dream to me. Being in flesh and bones in a piece of joined aluminum that I used to see only on TV or sometimes very far up there in the sky in the size of a grasshopper. I had never understood how that thing could carry people and fly them so far up above the lands. I had never understood how people would sit in this machine and not be scared for their lives. So many questions crossed my mind. These questions were now being answered, since I was now in the big flying "bird" myself. But let me tell you. I didn't think my mind was still in me.

I spoke to God and told Him: "If I die here, it is because you've wanted it." I told him: "Nothing is going to happen to us because I am in this plane, and I am going for a very important mission, to study your Word and take the Gospel to the nations of the earth." I was so confident, but needed to be guided.

It was so good to see that we were served food on board: soft drink and fruits. I would drink juice during the whole trip. Do you know that there was a restroom in the plane? I did not know. You want me to tell you if I went to the restroom. Well, I did not go. I don't remember I went. I don't think I went. I was afraid to fall while walking the isles to go the restroom, and I thought that my "mess" would fall off board. Yeah!

From time to time we were informed how many miles away we were from the ground and the number of miles we were still away from our destination. The weather forecast was also a part of the information we received from the monitors installed right behind each passenger's seat. From time to time I would put on the earphones and watch cartoons.

At our arrival at Roissy Charles de Gaulle we were welcome by a severe winter cold. I had never felt such a cold in my entire life. It was so cold that I did not feel I had my clothes on. I felt like I was in a freezer. Fortunately a bus came at once and we were taken to the lounge to wait for the next flight, which was scheduled at 10:30am that Sunday morning.

In the meantime we had to change our transfer and make sure we were waiting at the right terminal. I had to make sure that I had gathered all the right information. Thank God all went well while I was at Roissy.

I used to hear the name Roissy Charles de Gaulle when I was still in my home country and that sounded like such a wonderful, unreachable and dream-stimulating place. Our journalists never forgot to mention it while reporting the head of state's visit to France.

The beauty of Paris could already give me and idea or a glimpse of what the United States of America would look like. I was admiring the story buildings standing in a distance away from the airport where we were waiting. I enjoyed watching the beautiful sunshine that saluted my short stop that Sunday morning at Roissy.

Despite of the delay I would leave Paris at a reasonable time. I was thinking of the distance that now separated me from my country. I was a very long distance away from my family and friends. I started to be homesick. I was going to a land where I did not know anybody. Can you imagine going to a place where you will be a stranger to everyone? We had a very good flight from Paris to Atlanta.

I landed safely at exactly 6:30 pm at the Atlanta **Hartsfield International Airport** in a winter weather. Although I did not have a chance to look at it very well, I thought the Atlanta **Hartsfield International Airport** was a very big one.

After our plane landed we all left the plane and walked through a long tunnel, a kind of hallway. I was so surprised to see people walking very fast, even running. I did not know why. I started to walk fast myself. Later I realized that they were such in a hurry to be checked quickly and catch their next transfer or plane on time. So the only option was to run or walk very fast to join the line, which was already forming.

Conclusion

The motivation to write does not always come from the great ambitions someone has. Sometimes it only begins with a note from a friend and the help of God. It is up to us to grab the thought, hold tight unto it and take a step of faith and let everything out. I allowed the principle to unfold in the preparation of *On Wings of Promise.* And now you have certainly enjoyed the final result.

I talked about my country and especially the village where I was born, my family, my education and more importantly, how I knew for sure that I was going to heaven and be with God forever. It was all by the grace of God. His goodness and mercy have truly been following me. My traveling experience to the United States of America will always be a memorable experience and a testimony of God's grace. And I can't wait to share with you how it has been so far since my feet touched the "land flowing with milk and honey".

Notes

Bill and Vonette Bright

Founders of Campus Crusade for Christ, International
http://www.ccci.org/about-us/our-founders/index.aspx

-Cameroon

A virtual guide to Cameroon. Get an overview of Cameroon's art, culture, people, environment, geography, history, economy and its government. Beside a country profile with facts and figures, this page offers maps, statistics, weather information, and links to sources that provide you with information about this West central African nation, e.g.: official web sites of Cameroon, addresses of Cameroonian and foreign embassies, domestic airlines, local news, city- and country guides with extensive travel and tourism information on accommodation, tourist attractions, events and more.
http://www.nationsonline.org/oneworld/cameroon.htm
The History of Cameroon,
http://www.sfu.ca/archaeology/museum/ndi/History.html
 Here or there, Share your travel-publish photos, travel blogs and video of your trips. Let's inspire each other, http://www.hereorthere.com/places/ntui

Printed in the United States
137540LV00001B/16/P